Handy Wisconsin Genealogy Handbook

I0412027

Gary L. Morris

©2015 Gary L. Morris

ISBN-13: 978-1508416777

ISBN-10: 150841677X

Table of Contents

Notes

Genealogical Research in Wisconsin

There is a wealth of genealogical records and resources available for tracing your family history in Wisconsin. Because of the abundance of information held at many different locations, tracking down the records for your ancestor can be an ominous task. Don't worry though, we know just where they are, and we'll show you which records you'll need, while helping you to understand:

1. What they are
2. Where to find them
3. How to use them

These records can be found both online and off, so we'll introduce you to online websites, indexes and databases, as well as brick-and-mortar repositories and other institutions that will help with your research in Wisconsin. So that you will have a more comprehensive understanding of these records, we have provided a brief history of the "Badger State" to illustrate what type of records may have been generated during specific time periods. That information will assist you in pinpointing times and locations on which to focus the search for your Wisconsin ancestors and their records.

A Brief History of Wisconsin

During the 17th century, the Ojibwa, Fox, Potawatomi, Sauk, Kickapoo, and other tribes settled in Wisconsin. They engaged in hunting, fishing, and agriculture, but their attention turned to the fur trade when Europeans arrived in the area. The French were the first to explore the area, with Jean Nicolet landing on the shores of Green Bay in 1634, and twenty years later the fur traders Pierre Esprit Radisson and Médard Chouart des Groseilliers spent time exploring the northern parts of Wisconsin.

The explorer Louis Jolliet crossed and the Jesuit priest Jacques Marquette traversed the entire state in 1673, and soon the Jesuits established missions awhile the fur traders set up trading posts. After the French and Indian War the British took ownership of the area, ruling it as part of Quebec province for nine years from 1774 to 1783. Even after being ceded to the United States after the Revolutionary War, the area remained very British in nature, until 1816 when the Americans established forts at Prairie du Chien and Green Bay.

Wisconsin was made part of the Northwest Territory in 1787, and was subsequently incorporated into the Indiana Territory, the Territory of Illinois, and eventually the Michigan Territory. Lead mining brought an influx of white settlers in the early 1820's, a hearty bunch known as "Badgers" because many lived in holes they dug in the ground. After the Black Hawk War ended Indian resistance in 1832, many tribes such as the Winnebago were moved to reservations outside of the state, while others such as the Menominee, Ojibwa, and some eastern tribes were permitted to settle on reservations inside Wisconsin.

The Wisconsin Territory was formed in 1836 and initially included all of Iowa and Minnesota, along with a portion of the Dakotas. In 1838 the Dakotas, Minnesota, and Iowa became part of the Iowa Territory. The 1830's brought a land boom fueled by scores of Yankees from New England and Southerners, who would settle in mining country, migrating to the area. Both the economy and population expanded rapidly, and after endorsing statehood in 1846, Wisconsin became the 30th state on May 29, 1848.

Wisconsin supported the Union cause during the Civil War, and almost 100,000 men from the state fought on the union side, over 12,000 dying. After the Civil War Wisconsin continued to prosper, as lumbering, food processing, and dairying became major industries, and Milwaukee developed into an important industrial center.

Immigrants from Sweden, Denmark, Norway, and Finland were attracted to Wisconsin as early as 1839, and large numbers of Germans and Irish soon followed. The majority of foreign born people living in Wisconsin in 1850 were mostly English speaking, but within ten years they were outnumbered by Germans. Additional industrial development soon brought Hungarians, Lithuanians, Greeks, Italians, Belgians, and especially Poles, who continued to arrive steadily until the restriction of immigration in the early 1920's.

Important Genealogical Dates in Wisconsin History

1634 – Explored and partially settled by French fur traders and missionaries

1760 – Occupied by British Colonial forces

1763 – Ceded by France to Great Britain

1774 – Governed by British as part of Quebec

1783 – Ceded by Britain to US

1787 – Part of Northwest Territory

1800 – Part of Indiana Territory

1809 – Part of Illinois Territory

1818 – Part of Michigan Territory

1836 – Created as separate territory

1848 - Statehood

Famous Battles Fought in Wisconsin

There have not been many great military battles fought in Wisconsin, though there was one encounter on Wisconsin soil during the War of 1812, the **Siege of Prairie du Chien**. Although no battles were fought in the state itself, Wisconsin troops fought in over 500 encounters during the **Civil War**. Much fighting took place on Wisconsin soil between white settlers and the Native American tribes that made the state their home, most notably during the **Fox War**, **Winnebago War**, and the **Black Hawk War**.

Siege of Prairie du Chien:
http://www.prairieduchien.org/visitors/history.htm

Civil War: http://www.wisconsinhistory.org/civilwar/battles.asp

Fox War:
http://www.wisconsinhistory.org/dictionary/index.asp?action=view&term_id=9152&term_type_id=3&term_type_text=things&letter=F

Winnebago War:
http://www.wisconsinhistory.org/dictionary/index.asp?action=view&term_id=578&term_type_id=3&term_type_text=things&letter=w

Black Hawk War: http://lincoln.lib.niu.edu/blackhawk/

The battle accounts that exist can be very effective in uncovering the military records of your ancestor. They can tell you what regiments fought in which battles, and often include the names and ranks of many officers and enlisted men.

Common Wisconsin Genealogical Issues and Resources to Overcome Them

Boundary Changes: Boundary changes are a common obstacle when researching Wisconsin ancestors. You could be searching for an ancestor's record in one county when in fact it is stored in a different one due to historical county boundary changes.

The **Atlas of Historical County Boundaries** can help you to overcome that problem. It provides a chronological listing of every boundary change that has occurred in the history of Wisconsin.

Atlas of Historical County Boundaries:
http://publications.newberry.org/ahcbp/documents/WI_Consolidated _Chronology.htm#Consolidated_Chronology

Name Changes: Surname changes, variations, and misspellings can complicate genealogical research. It is important to check all spelling variations. Soundex, a program that indexes names by sound, is a useful first step, but you can't rely on it completely as some name variations result in different Soundex codes. The surnames could be different, but the first name may be different too. You can also find records filed under initials, middle names, and nicknames as well, so you will need to **get creative with surname variations** and spellings in order to cover all the possibilities. For help with surname variations read our instructional article on **How to Use Soundex**.

get creative with surname variations:
http://obituarieshelp.org/blog/?p=634

How to Use Soundex: http://obituarieshelp.org/blog/?p=505

Wisconsin Genealogical Organizations and Archives

Genealogical resources include not only records, but the organizations that house them, or can direct you to them. These institutions include: *Archives, Libraries, Genealogical Societies, Family History Centers, Universities, Churches, and Museums.*

Following are links to their websites, their physical addresses, and a summary of the records you can find there.

Archives and Libraries

Wisconsin Historical Society - One of the largest genealogical collections in the United States, contains: Cemetery records, Census records, Church records, Family Histories, Images, Immigration records, Local Histories, Maps, Military records, Naturalization records, Historical Newspapers, Vital records

816 State Street
Madison, WI 53706
Tel: 608-264-6460

Wisconsin Historical Society:
http://www.wisconsinhistory.org/genealogy/

University of Wisconsin at Green Bay - Vital Records, Citizenship Records, Court Records, Probate Record, Census Records, Land Records, School Records

UW-Green Bay, 2420 Nicolet Dr
Green Bay, WI 54311-7001
(920) 465-2539
archives@uwgb.edu

University of Wisconsin at Green Bay:
http://www.uwgb.edu/archives/

La Crosse Public Library Archives – Local histories, Obituaries, Vital records, Census records,

800 Main St.
La Crosse, WI 54601
Tel: (608) 789-7136
EMail: archives@lacrosselibrary.org

La Crosse Public Library Archives:
http://archives.lacrosselibrary.org/genealogy/genealogy-database/

University of Wisconsin - Madison - Genealogical information on former faculty, staff, and students

Library Archives
425 Steenbock Library
550 Babcock Drive
Phone: (608) 262-5629
Madison, WI 53706

Library Archives: http://archives.library.wisc.edu/genealogy.html

McIntyre Library - Federal and Wisconsin censuses, Pre 1907 vital records, Local government records, including naturalization, school, probate, tax, land, and court records (civil, criminal, and divorce), Church records and congregational histories, Diaries, letters, and organizational records, County and Local Histories, Genealogy Reference Books

University of Wisconsin-Eau Claire
Eau Claire WI 54702-4004
Reference Phone: 715-836-3858
Circulation Phone: 715-836-3856
FAX: 715-836-2949
EMail: library.reference@uwec.edu

McIntyre Library:
http://www.uwec.edu/Library/archives/genealogy/

University of Wisconsin - Stout Library – Local histories, Circuit/county courts, probates, naturalizations, and funerals between 1855 and 1955, Birth/death/probate notices from newspapers, 1862-1930

712 South Broadway St.
Menomonie, WI 54751
Tel: 715/232-1353
Email: reference@uwstout.edu

University of Wisconsin - Stout Library:
http://www.uwstout.edu/lib/archives/genealogy.cfm

Genealogical and Historical Societies

Genealogical and historical societies have access to extensive catalogues of genealogical data. They are also able to offer expert guidance for genealogical researchers. Many members are professional genealogists who are most willing to share their expertise in finding ancestors.

Wisconsin State Genealogical Society – Cemetery records, Surnames lists, and many more genealogical resources concentrating on research in specific counties

P.O. Box 5106
Madison, WI 53705-0106
E-mail: wsgs@wsgs.org

Wisconsin State Genealogical Society: http://wsgs.org/

Friends of Scandinavian History – Census records and many resources for tracing ancestors of Scandinavian ancestry in Wisconsin

P.O. Box 15
Scandinavia, WI 54977
Phone: (715) 467-2729
Email: scandinavia@tds.net

Friends of Scandinavian History:
http://www.friendsofscandinaviahistory.org/

German Interest Group - Wisconsin - Surnames lists and resources for tracing ancestors of German ancestry in Wisconsin

P.O. Box 762
Janesville, WI 53547-0762
Email:
gig.wi@hotmail.com

German Interest Group - Wisconsin: http://www.gig-wi.com/index.htm

Additional Wisconsin Genealogy Resources

Wisconsin Mailing Lists

Mailing lists are internet based facilities that use email to distribute a single message to all who subscribe to it. When information on a particular surname, new records, or any other important genealogy information related to the mailing list topic becomes available, the subscribers are alerted to it. Joining a mailing list is an excellent way to stay up to date on Wisconsin genealogy research topics. Rootsweb have an extensive listing of **Wisconsin Mailing Lists** on a variety of topics.

Wisconsin Mailing Lists:
http://lists.rootsweb.ancestry.com/index/usa/WI/misc.html

Wisconsin Message Boards

A message board is another internet based facility where people can post questions about a specific genealogy topic and have it answered by other genealogists. If you have questions about a surname, record type, or research topic, you can post your question and other researchers and genealogists will help you with the answer. Be sure to check back regularly, as the answers are not emailed to you. The Wisconsin message boards at **Rootsweb** are completely free to use.

Rootsweb:
http://boards.rootsweb.com/localities.northam.usa.states/mb.ashx

Wisconsin Newspapers and Periodicals

Many genealogy periodicals and historical newspapers contain reprinted copies of family genealogies, transcripts of family Bible records, information about local records and archives, census indexes, church records, queries, land records, obituaries, court records, cemetery records, and wills. The following sites have historical Wisconsin newspapers and periodicals that you can search online or on-site.

Wisconsin Historical Society - Approximately 4,000 Wisconsin and National newspapers dating from 17th century to present

816 State Street
Madison, WI 53706
Tel: 608-264-6460

Wisconsin Historical Society:
http://www.wisconsinhistory.org/genealogy/

GenealogyBank.com – free searchable database of Wisconsin newspaper archives, 1837-1992

GenealogyBank.com:
http://www.genealogybank.com/gbnk/newspapers/explore/USA/Wisconsin/

The Online Books Page – links to historical Wisconsin books and periodicals available for viewing online

The Online Books Page:
http://onlinebooks.library.upenn.edu/webbin/book/browse?type=subject&type=subject&key=wisconsin

NewspaperArchive.com – largest online database of historical newspapers in the world.

NewspaperArchive.com link to: http://newspaperarchive.com/

Historical Wisconsin Maps and Gazetteers

Maps are an integral part of genealogical research. They help us to locate landmarks, towns, cities, parishes, states, provinces, waterways and roads and streets. They also help us to determine when and where boundary changes might have taken place, and give us a visualization of the area we're researching in.

For locating place names, a gazetteer is the best possible resource for any genealogist. Gazetteers are also sometimes called "place name dictionaries", and can help you to locate the area in which you need to conduct research. Below are links to the maps and gazetteers for research in Wisconsin.

Peabody GNIS Service – Wisconsin;
http://peabody.research.yale.edu/cgi-bin/Query.GNIS?ST=Wisconsin&SU=1

Color Landform Atlas – Wisconsin:
http://fermi.jhuapl.edu/states/wi_0.html

1985 U.S. Atlas: http://www.livgenmi.com/1895/WI/

Wisconsin Hometown Locator:
http://wisconsin.hometownlocator.com/

Wisconsin City Directories

City directories are similar to telephone directories in that they list the residents of a particular area. The difference though is what is important to genealogists, and that is they pre-date telephone directories. You can find an ancestor's information such as their street address, place of employment, occupation, or the name of their spouse.

A one-stop-shop for finding city directories in Wisconsin is the **Wisconsin Online Historical Directories** which contains a listing of every available online historical directory related to Wisconsin. Another useful site is **US City Directories** which identifies printed, microfilmed, and online Wisconsin directories and their repositories.

Wisconsin Online Historical Directories:
https://sites.google.com/site/onlinedirectorysite/Home/usa/wi

US City Directories: http://www.uscitydirectories.com/wi.htm

University of Wisconsin Digital Collections - Online Madison city directories from 1858 – 1921

University of Wisconsin Digital Collections:
http://uwdc.library.wisc.edu/collections/WI

Wisconsin Genealogical Records

Birth, Death, Marriage and Divorce Records – Also known as vital records, birth, death, and marriage certificates are the most basic, yet most important records attached to your ancestor. The reason for their importance is that they not only place your ancestor in a specific place at a definite time, but potentially connect the individual to other relatives. Below is a list of repositories and websites where you can find Wisconsin vital records.

Wisconsin Center for Health Statistics - Births October 1, 1907 to present, Deaths October 1, 1907 to present, Marriages October 1, 1907 to present, Divorces October 1, 1907 to present

Dept. of Health and Social Services
P.O. Box 309
Madison, Wisconsin 53701
Wisconsin Center for Health Statistics:
http://www.dhs.wisconsin.gov/VitalRecords/

Wisconsin Historical Society - Births, 1852-September 30, 1907; Marriages, 1836-September 30, 1907; Deaths, 1852-September 30, 1907

816 State Street
Madison, WI 53706
Tel: 608-264-6460
Wisconsin Historical Society:
http://www.wisconsinhistory.org/genealogy/

University of Wisconsin at Green Bay - Statewide index to births, marriages, and deaths that were registered before 1907

UW-Green Bay, 2420 Nicolet Dr
Green Bay, WI 54311-7001
(920) 465-2539
archives@uwgb.edu

University of Wisconsin at Green Bay:
http://www.uwgb.edu/archives/

Family Search has the following indexes that can be searched online for free:

Wisconsin, Birth Index, 1820-1907:
https://familysearch.org/search/collection/1946789

Wisconsin, Births and Christenings, 1826-1926:
https://familysearch.org/search/collection/1708703

Wisconsin, Death Index, 1820-1907:
https://familysearch.org/search/collection/1940759

Wisconsin, Death Index, 1959-1997:
https://familysearch.org/search/collection/1947978

Wisconsin, Death Records, 1867-1907:
https://familysearch.org/search/collection/1803975

Wisconsin, Deaths and Burials, 1835-1968:
https://familysearch.org/search/collection/1708699

Wisconsin, Divorce Index, 1965-1984:
https://familysearch.org/search/collection/1967741

Wisconsin, Marriage Index, 1973-1997 :
https://familysearch.org/search/collection/1946794

Wisconsin, Marriages, 1836-1930:
https://familysearch.org/search/collection/1708704

Census Records

Census records are among the most important genealogical documents for placing your ancestor in a particular place at a specific time. Like BDM records, they can also lead you to other ancestors, particularly those who were living under the authority of the head of household.

Wisconsin Historical Society - United States Federal Census 1790-1920, Wisconsin State Census 1836-1905, Canadian Census 1666-1901

816 State Street
Madison, WI 53706
Tel: 608-264-6460
Wisconsin Historical Society:
http://www.wisconsinhistory.org/genealogy/

University of Wisconsin at Green Bay – Federal Census 1820 - 1940, State Ccensus 1836 - 1905, Native American Census Roll for Menominee, Oneida, Stockbridge, and Munsee Tribes 1885-1942

UW-Green Bay, 2420 Nicolet Dr
Green Bay, WI 54311-7001
(920) 465-2539
archives@uwgb.edu

University of Wisconsin at Green Bay:
http://www.uwgb.edu/archives/

La Crosse Public Library Archives – Wisconsin portion of United States census: 1850-1880, Wisconsin state census: 1855, 1875-1905

800 Main St.
La Crosse, WI 54601
Tel: (608) 789-7136
EMail: archives@lacrosselibrary.org

La Crosse Public Library Archives:
http://archives.lacrosselibrary.org/genealogy/genealogy-database/

The **Free Census Project** has transcribed many Wisconsin indexes and new material is added daily

Free Census Project: http://usgwcensus.org/cenfiles/wi.htm

Access Genealogy – Wisconsin county census records dating from 1810-1930

Access Genealogy:
http://www.accessgenealogy.com/census/wisconsin-census-records.htm

African American Census Schedules Online – slave schedules, mortality schedules, slave-owners census

African American Census Schedules Online:
http://www.afrigeneas.com/aacensus/

Native Americans in Census Records (US National Archives):
http://www.archives.gov/research/census/native-americans/

Wisconsin Church Records

Church and synagogue records are a valuable resource, especially for baptisms, marriages, and burials that took place before 1900. You will need to at least have an idea of your ancestor's religious denomination, and in most cases you will have to visit a brick and mortar establishment to view them.

Most church records are kept by the individual church, although in some denominations, records are placed in a regional archive or maintained at the diocesan level. Local Historical Societies are sometimes the repository for the state's older church records. Below are links archives that maintain church records, as well as a few databases that can be viewed online.

The **Family History Library** contains many church records from a variety of denominations on microfilm.

Family History Library:
http://familysearch.org/learn/wiki/en/Family_History_Library

McIntyre Library – Variety of Church records and Congregational histories dating from mid-19th century to present; includes; Lutheran, Episcopalian, Congregational, Catholic, Indian mission records, and more

University of Wisconsin-Eau Claire
Eau Claire WI 54702-4004
Reference Phone: 715-836-3858
Circulation Phone: 715-836-3856
FAX: 715-836-2949
EMail: library.reference@uwec.edu

McIntyre Library:
http://www.uwec.edu/Library/archives/genealogy/

Central Repositories for Denominational Records

Church of Jesus Christ of Latter-day Saints (Mormons)

Early Mormon Church records for Wisconsin can be found on film located at the LDS Family History Library in Salt Lake City and can be searched via the **Family History Library Catalog**

Family History Library Catalog:
https://familysearch.org/eng/Library/FHLC/frameset_fhlc.asp

The **Church History Library** has an even broader collection of historical church records than the Family History Library.

Church History Library
15 East North Temple
Salt Lake City, Utah 84150-1600
Phone: (801) 240-2272

Church History Library:
https://history.lds.org/?lang=eng#FlashPluginDetected

Baptist

American Baptist - Samuel Colgate Historical Library
1106 South Goodman Street
Rochester, NY 14620-2532
Phone: (716) 473-1740
Fax: (716) 473-1740

American Baptist - Samuel Colgate Historical Library:
http://abhsarchives.org/

Lutheran

Wisconsin Evangelical Lutheran Synod
Department of Archives and History
2929 North Mayfair Road
Milwaukee WI 53222
Phone: (414) 256-3888

Department of Archives and History: http://www.wels.net/

Presbyterian

Presbyterian Historical Society
425 Lombard Street
Philadelphia, PA 19147
Telephone: 1-215-627-1852
Fax: 1-215-627-0509

Presbyterian Historical Society: http://www.history.pcusa.org/

Methodist

Wisconsin Conference United Methodist Church
750 Windsor Street
Sun Prairie, WI 53590
Phone: (608) 837-7328

Wisconsin Conference United Methodist Church:
http://www.wisconsinumc.org/content/index.php

Roman Catholic

Archdiocese of Milwaukee
2000 West Wisconsin Avenue
Milwaukee, WI 53403
Phone: (414) 769-3300

Archdiocese of Milwaukee :
http://www.archmil.org/archmil/home.htm

Diocese of Green Bay
1910 South Webster Avenue
P.O. Box 66
Green Bay, WI 54301
Phone: (414) 435-4406

Diocese of Green Bay: http://www.gbdioc.org/

Diocese of La Crosse
421 Main Street
P.O. Box 982
La Crosse, WI 54601
Phone: (608) 788-7700

Diocese of La Crosse: http://www.dioceseoflacrosse.com/

Diocese of Madison
15 East Wilson Street, Box 111
Madison, WI 53701
Phone: (608) 256-2677

Diocese of Madison: http://www.madisondiocese.org/

Diocese of Superior
1201 Hughitt Avenue, Box 969
Superior, WI 54880
Phone: (715) 392-2937

Diocese of Superior: http://www.catholicdos.org/

Wisconsin Military Records

More than 40 million Americans have participated in some kind of war service since America was colonized. The chance of finding your ancestor amongst those records is exceptionally high. Military records can even reveal individuals who never actually served, such as those who registered for the two World Wars but were never called to duty.

Below are a number of links to websites and archives that contain Wisconsin military records.

Wisconsin Historical Society - Large variety of records such as Muster Rolls, Service records, Draft Registrations, Pensions Indexes etc. covering the Revolutionary War, War of 1812, Civil War, Spanish-American War, World War I, World War II, Korean War, and Vietnam War

816 State Street
Madison, WI 53706
Tel: 608-264-6460

Wisconsin Historical Society:
http://www.wisconsinhistory.org/genealogy/

National Archives and Records Administration - World War I Draft Registration Cards
Microfilm Roll List

8601 Adelphi Road
College Park, MD 20740-6001
Toll free: 1-866-272-6272

National Archives and Records Administration:
http://www.archives.gov/research/military/

US Department of Veterans Affairs Nationwide Gravesite Locator – includes information on veterans and their family members buried in veterans and military cemeteries having a government grave marker.

US Department of Veterans Affairs Nationwide Gravesite Locator: http://gravelocator.cem.va.gov/

You may also find your ancestor's military records in the following databases:

United States General Index to Pension Files, 1861-1934: https://familysearch.org/search/collection/1919699

United States Index to Service Records, War with Spain, 1898: https://familysearch.org/search/collection/1919583

United States Index to Indian Wars Pension Files, 1892-1926 – military pension records of soldiers who fought in the Indian Wars between 1817 and 1898

United States Index to Indian Wars Pension Files, 1892-1926: https://familysearch.org/search/collection/1979427

United States Registers of Enlistments in the U.S. Army, 1798-1914: https://familysearch.org/search/collection/1880762

United States Mexican War Pension Index, 1887-1926 - index to Mexican War pension files for service between 1846 and 1848

United States Mexican War Pension Index, 1887-1926: https://familysearch.org/search/collection/1979390

Civil War Soldiers Service Records - Service records for both Union and Confederate soldiers indexed by soldier's name, rank, and unit.

Civil War Soldier Service Records: http://go.fold3.com/civilwar_records/

Wisconsin Cemetery Records

As convenient as it is to search cemetery records online, keep in mind that there are a few disadvantages over visiting a cemetery in person. They are:

- Tombstone information is not always accurately transcribed
- The arrangement of the graves in a cemetery can be crucial as family members are often buried next to each other or in the same grave. This arrangement is not always preserved in the alphabetical indexes that are found online.

With that information in mind, the following websites have databases that can be searched online for Wisconsin Cemetery records.

Wisconsin Tombstone Transcription Project - death and burial records

Wisconsin Tombstone Transcription Project:
http://www.usgwtombstones.org/wisconsin/wiscon.html

Wisconsin Historical Society - Records from Wisconsin public and private cemeteries, Guyant Collection of Tombstone Inscriptions; includes tombstone inscriptions copied from seventeen Wisconsin counties

816 State Street
Madison, WI 53706
Tel: 608-264-6460

Wisconsin Historical Society:
http://www.wisconsinhistory.org/genealogy/

McIntyre Library – County cemetery records and transcriptions covering the entire state of Wisconsin

University of Wisconsin-Eau Claire
Eau Claire WI 54702-4004
Reference Phone: 715-836-3858
Circulation Phone: 715-836-3856
FAX: 715-836-2949
EMail: library.reference@uwec.edu

McIntyre Library:
http://www.uwec.edu/Library/archives/genealogy/

African American Cemeteries Online – African American, slave, and Native American cemetery records

African American Cemeteries Online:
http://africanamericancemeteries.com/

Access Genealogy – database of Wisconsin cemetery record transcriptions:
http://www.accessgenealogy.com/cemetery/wisconsin-cemetery-records.htm

Find a Grave – over 100 million grave records can be searched on this site. Search can be conducted by name, location, or cemetery name.

Find a Grave: http://www.findagrave.com/

Interment.net - A free online database containing approximately 4 million cemetery records from around the world:
http://www.interment.net/

Billion Graves – as the name implies, you can search a billion records including headstone photos, transcriptions, cemetery records, and grave locations.

Billion Graves:
http://billiongraves.com/pages/search/index.php#cemetery

Wisconsin Obituaries

Obituaries can reveal a wealth about our ancestor and other relatives. You can search our **Wisconsin Obituaries Listings** from hundreds of Wisconsin newspapers online for free.

Wisconsin Obituaries Listings:
http://obituarieshelp.org/wisconsin_newspaper_obituaries.html

Wisconsin Wills and Probate Records

The documents found in a probate packet may include a complete inventory of a person's estate, newspaper entries, witness testimony, a copy of a will, list of debtors and creditors, names of executors or trustees, names of heirs. They can not only tell you about the ancestor you're currently researching, but lead to other ancestors.

University of Wisconsin at Green Bay – County Probate records, 1821-1976

UW-Green Bay, 2420 Nicolet Dr
Green Bay, WI 54311-7001
(920) 465-2539
archives@uwgb.edu

University of Wisconsin at Green Bay:
http://www.uwgb.edu/archives/

McIntyre Library - County Probate records, 1854-1953

University of Wisconsin-Eau Claire
Eau Claire WI 54702-4004
Reference Phone: 715-836-3858
Circulation Phone: 715-836-3856
FAX: 715-836-2949
EMail: library.reference@uwec.edu

McIntyre Library:
http://www.uwec.edu/Library/archives/genealogy/

Family Search has the following indexes that can be searched online for free:

Wisconsin, Outagamie County Records, 1825-1980:
https://familysearch.org/search/collection/1463639

Wisconsin, Probate Estate Files, 1848-1948:
https://familysearch.org/search/collection/1874190

Wisconsin Immigration and Naturalization Records

The naturalization process generated many types of records, including petitions, declarations of intention, and oaths of allegiance. These records can provide family historians with information such as a person's birth date and place of birth, immigration year, marital status, spouse information, occupation, witnesses' names and addresses, and more.

If your ancestor lived in or near a large city, or near a city where U.S. courts convened, you may find naturalization records in the **U.S. District Court** before 1906.

U.S. District Court:
http://www.uscourts.gov/FederalCourts/UnderstandingtheFederalCo urts/DistrictCourts.aspx

Wisconsin naturalization records can be found in municipal, county, circuit, supreme, and United State territorial and district courts. Most naturalization records have been transferred from the Wisconsin court system to the Wisconsin Historical Society. Records from various jurisdictions have been brought together and are available for research at the Society's **Area Research Centers**.

Area Research Centers:
http://www.wisconsinhistory.org/libraryarchives/arcnet/

Wisconsin Historical Society - North American Passenger Lists, 1565 - 1954; Customs Passenger Lists, 1891-1954; Immigration Passenger Lists, 1991-1954

816 State Street
Madison, WI 53706
Tel: 608-264-6460

Wisconsin Historical Society:
http://www.wisconsinhistory.org/genealogy/

University of Wisconsin at Green Bay – County Naturalizations, 1848 - 1984

UW-Green Bay, 2420 Nicolet Dr
Green Bay, WI 54311-7001
(920) 465-2539
archives@uwgb.edu

University of Wisconsin at Green Bay:
http://www.uwgb.edu/archives/

US National Archives – Immigration records, Naturalization records, Ship's Passenger lists

The National Archives and Records Administration
8601 Adelphi Road
College Park, MD 20740-6001
Tel: 1-866-272-6272; 1-86-NARA-NARAS

US National Archives: http://www.archives.gov/research/guide-fed-records/groups/085.html

Family Search has the following indexes which can be searched online for free:

Wisconsin, County Naturalization Records, 1807-1992:
https://familysearch.org/search/collection/2046887

Wisconsin, Dane County Naturalization Records, 1887-1945:
https://familysearch.org/search/collection/1384564

Wisconsin, Milwaukee Naturalization Index, 1848-1990:
https://familysearch.org/search/collection/2138589

Wisconsin, Milwaukee Petitions to Naturalization, 1848-1991:
https://familysearch.org/search/collection/2174939

Wisconsin Native American Records

University of Wisconsin at Green Bay – Native American Census Roll for Menominee, Oneida, Stockbridge, and Munsee Tribes 1885-1942

UW-Green Bay, 2420 Nicolet Dr
Green Bay, WI 54311-7001
(920) 465-2539
archives@uwgb.edu

University of Wisconsin at Green Bay:
http://www.uwgb.edu/archives/

National Archives and Records Administration - Dawes Commission Final Cards of the Five Civilized Tribes

8601 Adelphi Road
College Park, MD 20740-6001
Toll free: 1-866-272-6272

National Archives and Records Administration:
http://www.archives.gov/research/military/

Access Genealogy – Wisconsin Native American census records, tribal histories, and much more

Access Genealogy:
http://www.accessgenealogy.com/native/wisconsin-indian-tribes.htm

U.S. National Archives - information on American Indians who maintained their ties to Federally-recognized Tribes (1830-1970).

U.S. National Archives: http://www.archives.gov/research/native-americans/

Records of the Bureau of Indian Affairs (BIA):
http://www.archives.gov/research/guide-fed-
records/groups/075.html

American Indians Records Repository - records dating from the
1700s including trust, education and other historic Indian Affairs
records

American Indian Records Repository
Meritex Enterprises
17501 West 98th Street
Lenexa, KS 66219
Phone: 913-888-0601

American Indians Records Repository:
http://www.doi.gov/ost/records_mgmt/american-indian-records-
repository.cfm

Missing Matriarchs – Resources for Researching Female Wisconsin Ancestors

Looking for female ancestors requires an adjustment of how we view traditional records sources. A woman's identity was often under that of her husband, and often individual records for them can be difficult to locate. The following resources are effective in locating female ancestors in Wisconsin where traditional records may not reveal them.

<u>Bibliographies</u>

- *On Wisconsin Women: Working for Their Rights From Settlement to Suffrage,* Genevieve G. McBride (University of Wisconsin Press, 1994)
- *Searching for your Wisconsin Ancestors in Wisconsin Libraries,* Betty Patterson (State Genealogical Society, 1977, 1987)
- *Sketches of Wisconsin Pioneer Women,* Florence Chambers Dexheimer (W.D Hoard & Sons, 1925)
- *The Uncommon Lives of Common Women: The missing Half of Wisconsin History,* Victoria Brown (Wisconsin Feminist Project Fund, 1975)
- *Dressing the Beds: Quilts and Coverlets from the Collection of the Milwaukee Public Museum,* Donald Hoke, (The Museum, 1985)
- *Wisconsin Women in the War Between the States,* Ethel Alice Hurn (Wisconsin History Commission, 1911)

Selected Resources for Wisconsin Women's History

McIntyre Library
University of Wisconsin-Eau Claire
Eau Claire WI 54702-4004
Reference Phone: 715-836-3858
Wisconsin Historical Society
816 State Street

FAX: 715-836-2949
EMail: library.reference@uwec.edu
Madison, WI 53706
Tel: 608-264-6460

Common Wisconsin Surnames

The following surnames are among the most common in Wisconsin and are also being currently researched by other genealogists. If you find your surname here, there is a chance that some research has already been performed on your ancestor.

Adams, Allen, Amy, Anderson, Ann, Asheim, Atterberry, Bagley, Baker, Banks, Barlow, Barnett, Barngrover, Beck, Bennett, Benton, Betty, Bice, Bobb, Boner, Brockus, Brown, Brubaker, Bullock, Bunton, Call, Campbell, Carr, Carson, Carver, Casebolt, Cassady, Catharine, Cerka, Chaffin, Chase, Clark, Clarke, Clough, Compton, Converse, Cook, Couse, Crisman, Culp, Curtis, Dabney, Davis, Dean, Dooley, Doolin, Eastburn, Eckles, Edwards, Emily, Etcheson, Etheridge, Evans, Everett, Farlin, Faulconer, Fenton, Fergerson, Ferguson, Flasher, Francis, Fry, Galpin, Gay, Geiher, Gibson, Gjeide, Gooden, Goodwin, Gotham, Graham, Grim, Grimes, Hagin, Hancock, Hannah, Happle, Harbin, Harris, Hatch, Henderson, Hildreth, Hinderlighter, Holmes, Homer, Hopkins, Hopkirk, Howell, Jackson, Jenalee, Johnson, Julina, King, Kinnick, Knapp, Langdon, Leach, Lee, Lindsay, Little, Lyman, Malcom, March, Margaret, Marion, Martha, Martin, Mary, Matthews, McFarland, McMain, McMains, McNelly, Meier, Mercy, Merrit, Merritt, Meyer, Michener, Miller, Mock, Moore, Myers, Norton, Owens, Paulson, Peterson, Phillips, Pirtle, Raburn, Raybourn, Rayburn, Reavis, Rector, Reuter, Rheinhardt, Rhodes, Richardson, Riddle, Ring, Roberts, Rogers, Rortvedt, Ross, Rowell, Runyon, Russell, Rymes, Schnee, Scott, Sheek, Sheila, Shookman, Shropshire, Sigourney, Slate, Sluder, Small, Smart, Smith, Snider, Somerville, Stevenson, Stilley, Stookesberry, Stump, Todd, Turk, Vaetch, Vanderford, Vanlandingham, Vaughn, Wager, Walker, Weeks, West, Wheeler, White, Whitman, Wilson, Wright, York

About the Author

Gary L. Morris worked from 2009 to 2014 as a professional researcher for a major player in the genealogy field. After tracing his family lineage back to 1683, he found that genealogy could be an expensive undertaking. As such, has decided to publish these helpful guides to share the valuable free information he has discovered during his career to help others trace their family lineages as inexpensively as possible. An avid genealogist himself, he hopes you will find this guide factual, thorough, helpful, and most of all, effective in helping you to find your family members.

Notes

Notes

www.ingramcontent.com/pod-product-compliance
Lightning Source LLC
Chambersburg PA
CBHW070510290526
45790CB00003B/1180